DOOM, DEATH & DANGER

D1469053

Read all the books in

THE HISTORY CHANNEL® PRESENTS
Series:

THE HISTORY CHANNEL® PRESENTS
HAUNTED HISTORY™:
AMERICA'S MOST HAUNTED

THE HISTORY CHANNEL® PRESENTS
HISTORY'S MYSTERIES®: BIZARRE BEINGS

THE HISTORY CHANNEL® PRESENTS
HISTORY UNDERCOVER®: TOP SECRET

THE HISTORY CHANNEL® PRESENTS
THE REAL SCORPION KING

THE HISTORY CHANNEL® PRESENTS
HAUNTED HISTORY™:
GHOSTLY GRAVEYARDS AND SPOOKY SPOTS

THE HISTORY CHANNEL® PRESENTS
HISTORY'S MYSTERIES®:
THE DEAD, THE DOOMED, AND THE BURIED

THE HISTORY CHANNEL® PRESENTS
MODERN MARVELS®: INVENTIONS THAT
ROCKED THE WORLD

THE
HISTORY
CHANNEL®
PRESENTS

★extreme™
history★

DOOM, & DEATH & DANGER

CIVIL WAR
SAMUEL BURLINGAME
Co. 3   C.V.H.A.
DIED AUG 28 1865
Æ   37

By Laurie Calkhoven

SCHOLASTIC INC.
New York   Toronto   London   Auckland   Sydney
Mexico City   New Delhi   Hong Kong   Buenos Aires

Cover designed by Louise Bova
Interior designed by Dawn Adelman

12 11 10 9 8 7 6 5 4 3 2 1   4 5 6 7 8/0

Printed in the U.S.A.
First printing, September 2004

Visit Scholastic.com for information about our
books and authors online!

CONTENTS

DOOM, DEATH & DANGER

DO ANYTHING TO STAY ALIVE!

It's dawn on September 10, 1813, when you hear the call: "All hands on deck!"

Six British warships have been spotted on the horizon and Commander Oliver Hazard Perry sees his chance to win back control of the Great Lakes from the Royal British Navy.

Walking on footropes attached to the 118-foot mast in pitching seas and in near dark, your fingers find the knots to release the ship's fifteen sails. Your shipmates hoist the USS *Lawrence's* two-ton anchor. Eight other ships in the U.S. fleet around you do the same thing.

There's time for a meal before you meet the enemy, and even though it's foul-tasting hardtack, you hope it won't be your last.

It takes six hours to reach the enemy and you tie up the lower sails so they won't catch fire before you man your post.

As the British warships concentrate their firepower on the *Lawrence*, cannonballs and bullets whiz past your ears. But you're still standing as splintering wood shatters around you.

By 2:30, there's a new order: "Abandon ship!" Along with four other men, you pile into a longboat with Commander Perry and head for the USS *Niagara*, dodging fire as you row to your sister ship.

Luckily, you make it to the *Niagara* unharmed and head back into dangerous battle. As the British *Detroit* and *Queen Charlotte* crash into each other, Commander Perry gives the order to continue fighting! In just fifteen minutes, the British surrender.

And you've managed to survive the danger! Welcome to Extreme History™, where the first rule of survival is: Do anything to stay alive!

Could you survive on what you could kill or

gather? Or make your way through dangerous terrain and rushing rapids? How about load a musket with bullets whizzing past your ear?

Throughout history, humans have had to struggle to survive. In prehistoric times, our ancestors were either the hunters or the hunted. Not only did they have to stalk giant beasts for dinner, but they also had to invent weapons and tools to kill and eat them!

Once humans learned how to fill their stomachs, they became curious about the world around them. Our American ancestors included daring explorers such as Lewis and Clark, who conquered the wilds of the West, and Major John Wesley Powell, who set off on a mission impossible to map America's last uncharted territory. No one had to fight harder to stay alive than the brave American soldiers who endured life-threatening battles at sea and on land.

Along the way, true American heroes were discovered — such as the cowboys who survived rattlesnakes and rushing rivers on the legendary

Chisholm Trail. And there were the heroes who had always been here — the Native Americans who created a proud lifestyle and survived for centuries hunting buffalo on the Great Plains.

Working with The History Channel®, we've uncovered some of our most exciting survival stories, when having the right tool — or a cast-iron stomach — was literally a matter of life and death. Read on to discover if you have what it takes to survive Extreme History™!

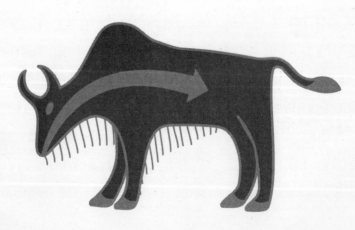

EAT OR BE EATEN

HOW PREHISTORIC PEOPLE SURVIVED

It's a good thing to be king of the beasts, and these days, that's exactly what we are. We're the hunters, not the hunted. But that wasn't always the case. Our early ancestors didn't have the bone-crushing jaws of the hyena or the razor-sharp claws and teeth of a saber-toothed tiger. But what they did have were brains, and that's where the story of ancient people's survival begins.

STANDING TALL

Over four million years ago, our earliest ancestors, the apelike *Australopithecus,* came down from the trees and walked upright. Two million years later, scientists believe, a new species arose: *Homo habilis.* Even though we'd probably run if we spotted one of these primitive humans on the street,

Homo habilis was more like you and me. He stood about four feet tall and, for his size, had a humongous brain.

My, Those Are Big Teeth You Have!

Because of his larger brain, *Homo habilis* noticed that there were other animals that could do things he couldn't do. For example, a hyena could break a bone with its jaws to get at the bone marrow. Not our idea of a delicious meal, but early humans didn't care much about keeping their elbows off the table or their napkins on their laps. They wanted to eat like hyenas!

The most important thing our ancestors discovered or invented was an axelike tool made of stone that historians call Oldowan choppers.

These stone choppers had sharp edges — sharper than fingernails and teeth. These tools made it possible for early humans to chop right through animal skin and bone to get to the marrow — the good stuff that was full of fat and protein. The choppers also had small, sharp flakes that could be used to scrape animal skins and slice meat.

SWITCH HITTERS

Let's fast-forward several hundred thousand years to when *Homo erectus* evolved (1.8 million years ago!). These early humans lived in Africa and began to populate the rest of the planet. And one reason they were able to thrive was because they carried tools we call hand axes. These axes were the first portable tool and a pretty fancy one! *Homo erectus* had studied rocks and discovered how to hit them at the right angles to get the sharpest blades.

EXTREME SURVIVAL

Evolution is the theory that all species of plants and animals developed from earlier forms of living things. It's the process through which plants and animals — including humans — change and develop. Scientists are still debating about how and where humans evolved and how they spread around the world, but most agree that we're related to these early humans.

The next thing our ancestors came up with was amazing — they switched from using rocks to what experts call a soft hammer, either bone or wood, which allowed *Homo erectus* to create a long, flat blade. "The easier to hunt you with, my dear!" said *Homo erectus* to his prey.

Grubbing for Grubs

Homo erectus were also known for using their brains. They used the horn of an antelope, the jawbone of a pig, and the teeth of a cat to dig with.

What did they dig for? Grubs! Early humans grubbed for grubs, another excellent source of protein that can be found in fallen trees and logs. When they were really lucky, they came across ant larvae! Aren't you glad you live in the age of fast food?

Fire

Although we take it for granted, discovering fire was a huge leap forward. Fire kept humans safe from predators. If you lit a fire in the mouth of your cave, no fierce beast would eat you for dinner! Early humans also used fire to cook the parasites out of their food (hey — that's mine, you worm!). At some point, they must have figured out that woolly mammoth tasted a lot better cooked than raw.

Historians don't really know where or how early humans discovered fire. They might have found it in the forest (sparked by lightning) or on their way to kill dinner, or maybe they learned to make fire by rubbing two sticks together.

For the first time humans could do one thing that no animal had done before: control their environment. Suddenly, men and women could use fire to turn winter into summer or night into day. And that helped them survive the next obstacle.

THINKING MAN AND WOMAN

About 40,000 years ago, the climate became colder and the Ice Age was on its way. As the animals died off, early humans had to invent new weapons to hunt for smaller and faster game. And of course, they were up to the survival challenge!

Hunting with Prehistoric Man

Over 100,000 years ago, a new species emerged. *Homo sapiens*, the thinking person, you and me. With a brain three times bigger than an ape, he was the first person to make weapons that could turn a little stone into a guided missile — in other words, a slingshot!

Now humans were no longer the weaklings of the wild. They were predators, hunting in packs and often stalking and tracking their next meal for days and days — until the animal finally lay down in exhaustion. Then the hunters used a spear to finish it off.

But remember — one wrong move and the hunter became the hunted.

As the big animals were dying off, *Homo sapiens* began to turn to smaller animals. Not only were there more of them, but their teeth were less ferocious and they didn't have to be tracked for days. But to kill these animals, our ancestors needed a different kind of tool. The slingshot — made with vegetable rope or animal hide and paired with a sharp rock — was the perfect answer.

Let's Go on Vacation!

Imagine you're a prehistoric man or woman, gazing out across the Zambezi River and wondering what's on the other side. Although it's only 200 yards away, no one's invented swimming yet. One day a log floats by and you have a brilliant idea!

SURVIVAL CHALLENGE:

Native cultures that track big game today catch their prey . . .

A. thirty percent of the time
B. fifty percent of the time
C. seventy percent of the time

Answer: thirty percent of the time. Our early ancestors probably had the same success rate.

The first big ocean-going migration began 40,000 to 60,000 years ago from Indonesia to Australia. The first boats and rafts were probably constructed of bamboo and plant fibers.

Humans were on the move. By 10,000 years ago, *Homo sapiens* had populated six of the seven continents of the world!

THE ICE AGE COMETH

In order to stay alive in the freezing temperatures, humans had to learn to make clothes and shelter — it was either do or die!

Technology Explosion!

When we think of technology, we think about computers and cell phones. But during the Ice Age, modern technology was actually a sewing needle. That's about the time *Homo sapiens* began using bones not just as weapons or digging tools, but to make fine tools like sewing needles (called awls) and harpoon points.

Early humans used stones to hammer small pieces of bone and ground them into long, sharp points. Then they punched a hole in the needle and threaded it with sinew. Pretty soon, our ancestors were wearing the latest fashions!

Home Sweet Home

Caves provided humans with shelter for hundreds of thousands of years, but as people moved north to colder climates, caves weren't always available. So if a human wanted to be king of the beasts, he had to build his own castle. Besides, man was on the move, and you can't take the cave with you.

A simple shelter, found in Africa, Australia, and even right here in America, was an A-frame house, made with branches gathered in the woods.

12

Did you know?
Early humans made clothes from animal skins, grass, and bark!

Early humans looked for notches and crotches to lock things together. Sticks, packed as closely as possible, made the walls. Leaves, bark, and pine needles kept out the sun and the rain.

In other parts of the world where it was really cold, early man built his house with the bones and tusks of giant mammoths and covered them with mammoth skins!

About 20,000 years ago (give or take a few years!), with basic inventions like tools and weapons, our early ancestors conquered the world. And because they didn't have to worry anymore about saber-toothed tigers, they were able to devote their brainpower to the things that make us truly human: creative thinking (hey, guys, how about a language!), art, science, and mapping our world.

Did you know?

Early man lit his shelter with stone lamps fueled by animal fat.

So the next time you turn on the TV, read an e-mail, or see a painting, remember to thank your great-great-great-great-great-great-great-great-great-great-great-great-great-great-great-great-great grandparents — who did anything to stay alive!

DARING QUESTS TO MAP AMERICA!

What was life like on the rugged quest to discover the American West? For the people who mapped America, there were no roads, no maps, and no drive-throughs! Whether they were trying to find a water route to the Pacific Ocean or attempting to map the West's last uncharted territory, the people who dared to conquer the wilds of the West had one rule of survival: Do anything to stay alive. Unfortunately, that also meant eating anything to stay alive!

SURVIVING THE LEWIS AND CLARK EXPEDITION

The year is 1804. The mission — to survive the Lewis and Clark expedition on their daring attempt to find a water route to the Pacific Ocean.

Like most people at the time, President Thomas Jefferson hoped there was a water connection between the Atlantic and Pacific Oceans. He turned to his young secretary, former army captain Meriwether Lewis, for help. Lewis recruited William Clark, a friend from his army days, to act as co-commander. The Corps of Discovery had just begun! Over the next four years they would travel thousands of miles.

What's That on My Plate?

The Lewis and Clark expedition left the Illinois territory on May 14, 1804. It was Lewis and Clark's last chance to gather supplies for the forty-five hunters, soldiers, and French boatmen in the Corps of Discovery. They stocked up on almost ten tons of provisions — including 3,000 pounds of pork and more than 5,500 pounds of flour. How would you like to carry that in your backpack?

It sounds like a lot of food, but it wasn't nearly enough. Along the way the explorers had to shoot buffalo, trap beaver, and catch fish for their supper. The expedition once caught 1,000 trout in two days! They ate 113 beavers — an average of one per week!

SURVIVAL STUNNER

The expedition discovered 122 species previously unknown to science, including the grizzly bear, the coyote, the California condor, and the gray wolf. Two bird species, Lewis's woodpecker and Clark's nutcracker, are named for the explorers!

When the expedition reached North Dakota, they built a fort and hunkered down for the winter. Their steady diet of game became scarce. But fortunately, the expedition included blacksmiths, and the Native American tribes in the area were big fans of hand-forged battle-axes. A single axe, with a treacherous fifteen-inch blade could be traded for as much as nine bushels of corn!

The men met and established peaceful contact

SURVIVAL CHALLENGE:

Which of the following did Lewis and Clark bring on the expedition as gifts for the Native Americans?

A. twelve dozen pocket mirrors
B. 4,600 sewing needles
C. vermilion face paint
D. all of the above

Answer: All of the above.

with fifty tribes during the expedition. Their most famous Native American friend was Sacagawea. She joined the Corps of Discovery with her French Canadian husband and baby son. Sacagawea helped the Corps as an interpreter and peacemaker.

Dude — Where's My Boat?

One of the first rules of water survival is to make sure your boat floats. Captain Lewis found that out the hard way. In an effort to limit the amount of gear that the men had to carry, or portage, Lewis designed the first steel collapsible boat. When his crew camped in North Dakota for the winter, he sent his biggest boat plus a dozen men back home. Big mistake! Cut to Great Falls, Montana. After a three-week portage, the men planned to attach elk skins to the iron frame of the boat and float west. But to do that, they needed resin, or pitch, from a pine tree, and there were no pine trees! The Corps of Discovery had to craft their own dugout canoes.

It took the men just under a week to make two canoes, chopping from sunup to sundown. Paddling those big, heavy canoes was kind of like

EXTREME SURVIVAL

Lewis's collapsible iron-frame boat weighed only ninety-nine pounds. Dugout canoes weighed an average of 2,000 pounds. Try carrying that over a mountain!

paddling a giant log down a river, and for part of the journey, the Corps had to paddle upstream!

Is That Food?

Things got even trickier when they reached the Rocky Mountains. No one knew how high the mountains were and how long it would take them to get to the other side. Supplies were running out, and the men had to find food to survive.

Hunger made the

SURVIVAL CHALLENGE:

The expedition put sails on their canoes and let the wind drive them the rest of the way west. True or false?

Answer: False. They tried putting sails on the canoes, but the wind was usually against them!

19

men do some crazy things — they even chewed wax and pretended it was food. But Captain Lewis was determined to do anything to stay alive, so the first cup of soup was born. The recipe:

Take one big pot and throw in some wild vegetables. Then add hooves and all the other gross parts of the animal that no one wants to eat. Boil it down to little flat squares and let it get hard. Days later, drop that hard square into a cup of boiling water and, presto, it's a meal. The men called it portable soup. It smelled bad and tasted even worse!

Although Lewis and Clark never did find a Northwest Passage, they reached the Pacific Ocean in November of 1805 and built Fort Clatsop in Oregon before returning to Missouri in September of 1806. Along the way (all 8,000 miles of it!), they discovered geography, plants, and animals of the Western frontier. Their daring journey paved the way for other courageous and dangerous missions.

More than sixty years later, another expedition set out to

SURVIVAL CHALLENGE:

Lewis and Clark never did find a Northwest Passage. True or false?

Answer: True. There isn't one!

Did you know?
Clark once went twelve days without anything to eat but grapes and one rabbit.

map the West — this time the treacherous Colorado River.

SURVIVING THE COLORADO RIVER EXPEDITION

The year is 1869. The mission — to survive the Powell expedition down the raging rapids of the Colorado River and map one of America's last uncharted territories.

The ten men of the Colorado River expedition pushed off from Green River Station, Wyoming, on May 24, 1869. Neither Major John Wesley Powell nor his crew of Civil War veterans and mountain men had a clue as to what to expect.

Does That Thing Float?

Powell and his men used clunky, wobbly wooden boats that weighed almost 1,000 pounds, and in order to get them to float you had to sink them! The theory was that if you sank them in the river for about a week, the boards would swell and tighten up, making the boats more waterproof.

After Powell's men bailed the boats out, they filled them with 7,000 pounds of food and equipment!

As they careened three hundred miles downstream, the Green merged with the Colorado River, and from that point on, the map was a blank!

Did you know?

The four boats were named: *Emma Dean, Kitty Clyde's Sister, Maid of the Canyon,* and *No Name.*

Two Strikes and . . .

The expedition had two strikes against it from the beginning. None of the men had ever navigated rapids before, and Powell himself couldn't row a boat. You see, Powell was a former Union artillery captain in the Civil War, and he got shot at the Battle of Shiloh, costing him his right arm.

Soon this inexperienced group was paddling backward down rapids in their heavy, unstable boats. To find out where they were going, they had to look over their shoulders. Luckily, you can hear the roar of the rapids long before you reach them.

Powell quickly learned that he needed somebody to steer with a rudder at the back of the boat, especially through the rapids. Wooden boats break, and the last thing they wanted was to hit a rock!

But that didn't help the men of the *No Name.* Just sixteen days into the trip, the men in the *No Name* misread Powell's signals. Instead of pulling into shore, the boat careened down huge rapids and hit a rock, pitching the men and most of their supplies into the river. The men were saved, but the supplies were lost!

Scaling the River Walls

For the men of the Powell expedition, there was nothing more exciting than white water. But Powell's main mission was to map the Colorado River, and in order to do that he had to hoist himself up on bluffs more

SURVIVAL CHALLENGE:

What did Powell name the spot where he lost the *No Name*?

A. Disaster Falls
B. Destruction Rapid
C. No Name Lost

Answer: A.

than 2,000 feet above the river. And he did it all with one hand!

Once his quest almost claimed his life. One day Powell was hundreds of feet above the ground, clutching on to a rock with his only hand and no footholds. With seconds to spare, one of Powell's men scrambled to a ledge just above. It was a life-and-death situation, and the man did the only thing he could do: He took off his clothes, lowered his long underwear to Powell, and pulled him up!

Powell's Muddy River Bread

The men complained in their diaries that while Powell was wandering around above them, seeming to have fun, they were left down on the ground doing the expedition's dirtywork — cooking dinner.

There's only so much you can do with soggy beans and rancid bacon. But after a while, even that was gone. So the men invented muddy river bread, with moldy flour, a little salt, and some ran-cid bacon fat. Sound yummy? Well, wait until you add the muddy water of the Colorado River and bake it in a Dutch oven over hot coals.

THE
HISTORY
CHANNEL

Also known as early cavepeople, *Homo sapiens* were the first humans to make weapons. They populated six continents in the world. True survivors!

In 1804 Lewis and Clark made a daring attempt to find a water route to the Pacific Ocean. Alas, they never found it.

Culver Pictures

Captain Perry was ordered to fight the British on Lake Erie. He gathered the bravest of sailors and defeated the British — hands down.

THE HISTORY CHANNEL

With casualties on both sides, Civil War soldiers did whatever it took to stay alive. During the war, three out of four operations were amputations of legs and arms!

Buffaloes were not only a source of food for Native Americans but also a means of survival. Buffalo skins were used to make clothes and shelter.

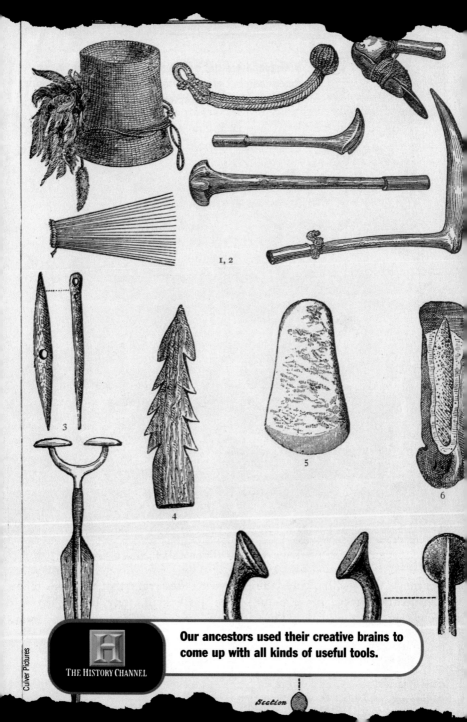

I, 2

3

4

5

6

THE HISTORY CHANNEL

Our ancestors used their creative brains to come up with all kinds of useful tools.

Section

John Wesley Powell set out to map the Colorado River with one arm and no boating experience. Total dedication!

THE HISTORY CHANNEL

From the days of the cavepeople to wartime battles, our ancestors proved that with skill and fierce determination we can survive anything that comes our way. The future looks bright.

Powell paid the men extra to kill wild game, but there wasn't much of it to hunt. By the end of the trip even the bacon fat was gone, and the men were reduced to making bread from just flour and water, called hardtack.

Lining the Rapids

To protect the boats and supplies from the dangers of the rapids, Powell ordered the men to carry both along the river's edge. They called it portaging, and it was the worst job on the whole expedition. Those boats were heavy!

To avoid the biggest rapids and spare their backs, the men invented "lining." With one man

LAW OF SURVIVAL

The men got so hungry that they even tried to eat wild potato greens. The potato greens must have looked good to the starving men, but looks can be deceiving. Not only did the potato greens make the men sick, they also made them see things that weren't there!

upstream on a rope, and another downstream, two or more men stood in the freezing-cold water holding on to the rope with one hand and the boat with the other. The boats were "lined" down the shoreline to keep them under control and protect them from hitting the rocks too hard. It was a treacherous job, and one the men had to do more than one hundred times.

Up a Creek without a Paddle

The boats weren't the only thing getting beat up by the rapids and the rocks — that was true for the oars as well. Whenever they found a big log, the men carved new oars to replace the ones that had been lost or broken.

By the time the expedition entered the Grand Canyon, the crew was losing its patience with Powell. The men were on the brink of mutiny and about to navigate the biggest, roughest rapids.

John Wesley Powell, who eventually helped found the National Geographic Society, became a national hero. His Colorado River expedition made Americans believe that the West was truly open and theirs for the taking.

LAW OF SURVIVAL

Powell and his men completed the 900-mile expedition — a humongous task — in just ninety-nine days. On the ninety-seventh day, three men left and began hiking out of the canyon. They were never seen or heard from again. Powell later called the spot Separation Canyon.

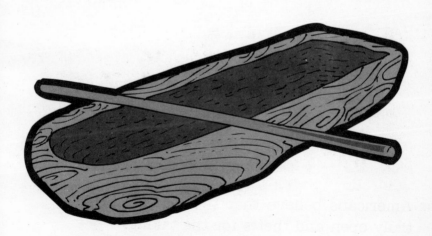

③ SURVIVING COMBAT

ON SEA AND ON LAND!

From the American Revolution to World War II to the war in Iraq, U.S. soldiers have always had what it takes to fight for freedom and survive extreme history.

Let's weigh anchor and set sail with Captain Perry's sailors in a legendary battle with the British, and live the hard-knock life of a Civil War soldier, when the first rule of survival was: Do anything to stay alive!

SURVIVING ON A WAR OF 1812 BATTLESHIP

The year is 1813. The mission: to survive Captain Oliver Hazard Perry's legendary battle with the British on Lake Erie.

In the early 1800s, no American ship was safe on the high seas. Great Britain, still smarting from its loss in the American Revolution, seized U.S. ships and cut off trade at every opportunity. Finally, the United States got tired of being bullied and declared war on the English. Even though we had won the Revolutionary War, it was still like a mouse declaring war on a lion!

Unfortunately for us, the lion roared back, sweeping down from Canada and capturing the most important forts on the Great Lakes. America was in need of a hero, and U.S. Navy Captain Oliver Hazard Perry was up to the job!

Building a Fleet!

Believe it or not, on the wild frontier of America, ships were the fastest way to move an army. So in March of 1813, the U.S. Navy ordered Captain Perry to challenge the British on Lake Erie. Perry had been a sailor since he was thirteen, and he knew his way around a ship. The only problem — he didn't have a fleet or a crew!

From his home base in Erie, Pennsylvania, the twenty-seven-year-old captain put together a ragtag crew of shipwrights (ship's carpenters), farmers, soldiers, and militiamen. He taught them the difference between a sheep and a sheepshank.

LAW OF SURVIVAL

Perry's sailors could tie one hundred knots — including the sheepshank, used to shorten the lines; the figure eight, which stopped the rope from slipping out to sea; and the bowline knot, used to hoist tools and supplies to the sailors up on the masts. There were ten miles of rope on an 1812 battleship. Without those lines — and the knots in them — the ship couldn't sail.

LAW OF SURVIVAL

Perry's fleet consisted of three brigs — the *Lawrence*, the *Niagara*, and the *Caledonia* — and six schooners.

On September 10, 1813 — only eight months after declaring war — the Americans had built six ships. That brought the total naval fleet to nine. Perry and his men were floating in Put-in-Bay, Ohio, on Lake Erie when he spotted six British warships ten miles away. Now was the time to test his fleet and his crew's training.

ANCHORS AWAY!

Getting a fighting brig under way was no small feat. First the men had to weigh, or pull up, the two-ton anchor. Then, following orders from the captain and his officers, twenty-four of the 155-man crew had to go aloft — walking on footropes and holding on to anything that didn't move — to unfurl the ship's fifteen sails! The main mast was 118 feet high and there were no safety harnesses. The

LAW OF SURVIVAL

During battle, lower sails were tied up so they wouldn't catch fire!

sailors not only had to climb up in the dark, but in pitching seas!

One Last Meal!

After sighting the British at dawn, the men had time for one meal — they all hoped it wouldn't be their last. Perry's men mostly ate salted meats and

LAW OF SURVIVAL

Square plates stow a lot better on a ship than round ones. Sailors were promised "three squares a day" while on board. That's where the phrase "square meal" comes from.

hardtack — a hard biscuit.

You would think that having enough freshwater wasn't a problem on Lake Erie, but the ships often anchored in calm seas, so the sewage of the entire fleet contaminated their drinking water. On the day they

SURVIVAL CHALLENGE:

Perry's sailors were ordered to get a good night's sleep before battle. True or false?

Answer: False! Back then, sailors slept in two shifts, getting just three and a half hours of shut-eye at a time!

sailed to face the British, foul water had made a quarter of Perry's men sick with dysentery. When they weren't running to the bathroom, they were lying in their hammocks — groaning!

Perry's fleet blockaded British supply lines, forcing them to either fight or starve. The U.S. fleet prepared for battle by spreading sand on the deck for better footing when the blood started to flow.

Don't Give up the Ship!

Perry's battle flag on the *Lawrence* was decorated with the motto "Don't Give up the Ship," but it didn't take long before the battle took a turn for the worse. After just two hours, the *Lawrence* had been battered by the British and eighty percent of Perry's crew was either killed or wounded. But Perry wasn't done yet. He still had eight other battleships, and he was willing to do anything to stay

LAW OF SURVIVAL

As many as one-fourth of the sailors who manned the U.S. squadron during the bloody Battle of Lake Erie were African-American.

alive — even if it meant abandoning ship!

Perry and five men piled into a longboat and made a daring dash, dodging cannon-balls, for the *Niagara*. He may have given up the ship, but he didn't give up the fight.

"We have met the enemy and they are ours."

By sheer luck, Perry made it to the *Niagara* and headed straight toward the British ships *Detroit* and *Queen Charlotte*. The badly damaged ships maneuvered to face the *Niagara* but crashed into each other instead! After just fifteen minutes of fire from the *Niagara*'s eighteen powerful car-ronades, the British surrendered. For the first time in history, the mighty Royal British Navy lost an entire fleet in battle. The first sentence of Perry's report to General (and later President) William Henry Harrison — "We have met the enemy and they are ours" — has become a famous quote in American history.

Unfortunately the next war U.S. soldiers would

have to fight was not against another country, but against each other.

SURVIVING COMBAT IN THE CIVIL WAR

The years are 1861 to 1865. The mission — to walk in the boots of a Civil War soldier.

In the North, the Civil War was about freeing the slaves and preserving the Union. But in the South, it was about states' rights. Soldiers struggled to find food and tried to keep cool in the face of battle.

Manual of Arms

Imagine if someone gave you a uniform, taught you how to march, stuck a gun in your hand, and then sent you off to war. That's what it was like during the Civil War, when soldiers trained for as little as three weeks before they were thrown into battle!

Both sides drilled their tired soldiers in between battles to finish the job of training. There was one maneuver that the soldiers had to practically learn in their sleep — the Manual of Arms. There were nine steps of loading and priming a rifle-musket before it was even ready to shoot. Try that with bullets whizzing past your ear! A seasoned soldier — one who had survived a battle or two — could fire off three shots a minute.

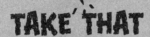

When the war began, the Union army had 16,000 men signed up for five years of duty. President Lincoln knew he needed more soldiers, so he asked for volunteers. In addition to American volunteers, thousands of men from Germany,

TAKE THAT

Yankees often yelled curses at the Rebs across the battlefield and the Rebs yelled back. Two of the names they called each other were "dandy sprat" and "dwiddlepoop"!

Ireland, France, Spain, Great Britain, and Italy served in the Union army and navy. Native Americans, including Creeks, Cherokees, and Seminoles, formed whole Southern regiments.

Fair Fight?

At the beginning of the war, firearms were in short supply. The guns issued to soldiers varied greatly —

SURVIVAL CHALLENGE:

When not in battle, the bayonet was a handy
A. candleholder
B. coffee grinder
C. tent pitch
D. all of the above

Answer: D — all of the above.

they included rifles, muskets, carbines, pistols, and shotguns.

Eventually, the average foot soldier carried a muzzle-loading rifle-musket. It had a sharp bayonet on the muzzle for close combat.

Many of the weapons given to Northern soldiers were more accurate and had a longer range than the Southern soldiers' muskets — meaning the Yanks could shoot from farther away and had a better chance of hitting their target. But the muskets and rifles were big enough to give men on both sides a case of the shakes — most of them weighed about eight-and-a-half pounds.

EXTREME SURVIVAL

Both the Confederate and Union armies used the same 1855 training manual. Its author became a Confederate general!

Most of the men who lost an arm or a leg in the war got hit with a minié ball. It shot out of the barrel with a lot more speed than a musket ball and did a lot more damage to the guy on the other side.

Surviving the Surgeon's Knife

During the Civil War, three out of every four operations involved the amputation of an arm or a leg. Surgeons performed more than 60,000 amputations before the war was over. Most doctors had only eight to ten minutes for any one patient and surgery was usually performed in a crude field hospital, sometimes on operating tables made from a few boards laid over barrels. As soon as an amputation was complete, the soldier was moved so another could take his place. By the end of a really bloody battle, a surgeon might have seen a thousand patients and would be standing knee-deep in blood and gore!

Weevils for Dinner, Anyone?

Soldiers lived mostly on hardtack, a hard cracker made from flour and water. Soldiers called it

SURVIVAL CHALLENGE:

What percentage of Civil War amputees survived?
A. ten percent
B. fifty percent
C. seventy-five percent

Answer: C — seventy-five percent

38

LAW OF SURVIVAL

More soldiers died from diseases like measles, malaria, and typhoid than from battlefield wounds.

"teeth dullers," "worm castles," and "sheet-iron crackers." Talk about a jawbreaker! Hardtack was designed to last a long time, not for its taste. The salt kept mice and cockroaches away, but it attracted weevils, which lived and laid their larvae in the crackers. Soldiers dunked, soaked, and crumbled hardtack in their coffee or soaked it in water until it was soft enough to fry in bacon grease. Food rations also included sow belly, salt pork, beans, and molasses.

Hay Is for Horses

Soldiers on both sides of the war rarely had fresh fruits or vegetables, which caused health problems, including a disease called scurvy. Thus the Union army invented the first dehydrated vegetable. Soldiers were issued dehydrated cakes of

beans, beets, carrots, onions, turnips, and other vegetables. The troops quickly nicknamed it "baled hay," not just because it looked like hay, but because it tasted like it, too!

Did you know?

The first potato chip? Union soldiers were sometimes issued potatoes, which they sliced thin and fried in bacon grease. They called them camp potatoes, but we might call them potato chips!

Getting fresh food was even harder for Confederate soldiers. Southern General Stonewall Jackson sucked on lemons to avoid scurvy.

EXTREME SURVIVAL

Even though it was against orders, many soldiers kept pets with them, including dogs, cats, squirrels, raccoons, and other wildlife. One regiment from Wisconsin had a pet eagle! And General Robert E. Lee had a pet hen who laid an egg under his cot every morning.

40

As the war dragged on, many Southern soldiers suffered from malnutrition and even starvation. The Union blockade kept ships away from Southern ports, and farmland and railroad lines were lost or destroyed in battle. By the war's end, flour could cost as much at $1,000 per barrel.

History at Its Most Extreme

Life was certainly extreme for Civil War soldiers. Being in the army meant months and months away from home, long hours of training between battles, terrible food, and often no shelter. A soldier spent days marching on hot, dusty roads or in the pouring rain, carrying everything he needed on his back.

More soldiers died in the "War Between the States" than in all other American wars combined.

What we know today about the average seaman from the War of 1812 and the Civil War soldier was handed down from diaries and history books. These men were young, scared, and far from home. They were worried about protecting the friend next to them and about beating the enemy. They had what it took to survive and stay alive!

④

STAYING ALIVE IN THE WILD, WILD WEST!

By the end of America's bloody Civil War, almost no cattle survived east of the Mississippi River. Union and Confederate soldiers had eaten most of them, and Americans missed their steaks and hamburgers!

In Texas, there was a totally different problem. During the war, the untended herds had grown bigger and bigger, and millions of Texas longhorns roamed the ranches. A steer could sell for as much as fifty dollars in the East, but in Texas, ranchers were lucky to get even three dollars!

The year is 1867. The mission — to survive a cattle drive on the legendary Chisholm Trail and live the rough-and-tumble life of a real American cowboy.

LET'S MAKE A DEAL

Texas cattlemen needed to find a way to sell their cattle in the East. Joseph McCoy, a promoter, had an idea. He worked out a deal with the Kansas-Pacific Railroad to build cattle pens and a new hotel in the railroad town of Abilene, Kansas, where the cattle could be shipped east.

To reach McCoy's shipping yard, cattle drivers used a route blazed by Jesse Chisholm, a part-Scottish, part-Cherokee trader who hauled goods for his trading posts across present-day Oklahoma.

EXTREME SURVIVAL

Over the years, the trail was known by various names, including the Abilene Trail, the Great Texas Cattle Trail, and McCoy's Trail. But Chisholm Trail is the name that stuck.

Texas cowboys in search of fame and fortune drove their cattle along the 900-hundred mile trail — stretching from Texas through Indian country to the rail yards of Abilene. You might say that the Chisholm Trail was America's first superhighway!

THE CATTLE DRIVE

Any cattle drive began with a roundup from the open range. Cows without brands had to be branded, and the cowboys had to get the cattle into one controllable herd. Once the cattle were in place, the cowboys manned their posts. On a cattle drive, every single cowboy had a specific job to do.

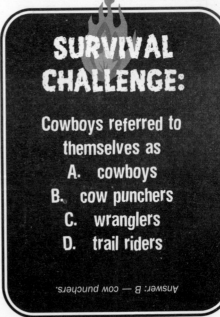

The trail boss was in charge of the cowboys and the cows. He rode in front of the herd. Behind him were the point men. Their job was to guide the cattle in the right direction and to search for water. Swingmen and flank riders had the toughest job on the range — keeping the cattle moving in the right direction and mak-

SURVIVAL CHALLENGE:

Cowboys referred to themselves as

A. cowboys
B. cow punchers
C. wranglers
D. trail riders

Answer: B — cow punchers.

ing sure they didn't stray. Finally, there were the drag riders — the guys in the dust at the rear who slowly pushed the cattle forward. That was the worst and dirtiest job on the trail, and usually was given to new guys, called greenhorns or greenies. Drive teams also included a wrangler, who was in charge of the extra horses.

The day lasted from sunup to sundown, with a rest stop at noon. For an average herd of about 2,500 cattle there were only eight to twelve cowboys! To stay awake for twelve hours on a horse, cowhands rubbed tobacco in their eyes!

EXTREME SURVIVAL

Almost one in three cowboys was either Mexican or African-American. A few adventurous women made the journey, sometimes disguised as boys!

A cowboy usually had just one change of clothes to last the entire four months on the trail. To get rid of lice, they put their shirts and pants on anthills. After the ants carried off the lice, they killed the ants!

45

Stop That Cow!

The biggest threat to a cowboy's survival on the trail was a stampede. Anything from lightning to a cowboy's sneeze could send frightened cattle charging in every direction. Once a thunderstorm near Waco, Texas, caused a herd of 15,000 long-horns to plunge into a steep ravine, killing several thousand cattle and injuring many cowboys.

Cowboys had to be both courageous and expert riders to round up stampeding cattle. If their horses stumbled, it often meant death for both the horse and the cowboy under the thundering hooves of stampeding cattle.

And it wasn't just stampedes — cowboys also had to worry about lightning, blizzards, and prairie fires. And then there were scorpion stings, snakebites, and Native American attacks! Work as a cowboy was dangerous — and there weren't any cell phones or hospitals for when a cowboy

SURVIVAL CHALLENGE:

Cowboys surrounded their bedrolls with rope at night, to keep the rattlesnakes away. True or false?

Answer: True! Rattlers have sensitive bellies and didn't like slithering over the rough bristles on the cowboys' hemp ropes.

46

was injured on the range. He either survived or was buried along the way.

River Crossings

River crossings killed even more cattle than stampedes. There were six major rivers to cross on the Chisholm Trail. When the rivers were low, cattle got caught in mud and quicksand. But when the water was high, cattle had to swim across. A single cow, struggling in midstream, could cause a panic — knocking cowboys off their horses and sending them to their deaths!

Crossing the Red River carried even more dangers than your usual river crossing. The Red River marked the border between Texas and Indian Territory, and the Indians had earned their reputation as skilled warriors.

Mostly, the Native Americans were helpful to the cowboys, leading them to water sources and guiding them across rough river crossings. Native Americans saw the cattle herds as a source of food and respect, especially when the animals crossed their land. Most of the time, owners were happy to pay for supplies in either cash or cattle. But when they didn't, the Native Americans would cause a stampede, stealing horses and cattle in the chaos that followed.

Cowboys had to be masters of the lariat — a

long piece of rope with a big loop at one end, used for catching cattle. With his lariat, a 150-pound cowhand could capture a 1,000-pound steer! Roping cattle was so important that cowboys practiced on feed sacks and hay bales until they were experts.

Chuck Wagon

On the trail, cowboys survived on the three b's — beef, beans, and bread. When they got hungry for something different, they hunted for rattlesnake! The cook and his chuck wagon rode miles ahead of the herds to make sure the meals and coffee were ready for the hungry cowboys at the end of the day.

Cooks were known to be cranky old cowhands, and it wasn't a good idea to complain about their food. Critics were rewarded with the smallest biscuits and the last of the beans scraped from the bottom of the pan!

Nothing was ever wasted on the trail. One of the cowboys' favorite meals was a stew made from the heart, tongue, liver, kidney, brain, and sweetbreads of the cow. The cowboys gave this stew a name we can't even print in this book!

Animal parts weren't the only things that didn't go to waste — food was cooked over a stinky fire of cow patties! The cook's assistant had the job of gathering them along the way. Not only were cow patties more plentiful than wood, they burned hotter and cooked faster than firewood!

Is There a Doctor in the House?

Cooks didn't just rustle up grub for hungry cowboys — they were also the closest thing to a doctor on a cattle drive. They couldn't stop by the nearest drugstore for some first-aid cream, so they made medicine from prickly pears! First they burned off the sharp points from the skin, then mixed the soft middle of the pear with goat tallow. It was an all-purpose cure — for saddle sores, rope burns, and even rattlesnake bites!

Cooks were so important that new

SURVIVAL CHALLENGE:

Cooks were the highest-paid men on the trail
True or false?

Answer: False! Cooks were the second-highest paid. Trail bosses were paid more.

SURVIVAL CHALLENGE:

Rattlesnakes can strike after they're dead.
True or false?

Answer: True! Rattlesnakes have been known to strike for as long as an hour after they're dead.

cowhands quickly learned the first rule of the trail: "Only a fool argues with a skunk, a mule, or a cook."

THE WILDEST TOWN IN THE WEST

Living on the trail was hard, dirty, tiring work. Cowboys were awake before dawn to get the herd ready for the day's march. They endured the heat, dust, wind, and weather (not to mention prairie dog holes!) and crossed dangerous rivers with frightened cattle, only to roll up in a blanket on the ground at the end of the day for a few hours of sleep.

Most cowboys weren't the deadly gunfighters that the old movies made them out to be. On cattle drives, cowboys kept their pistols in their saddlebags. And because most of them didn't even have holsters, when they went to town, they wore their pistols in their belts.

EXTREME SURVIVAL

A Colt revolver cost twelve dollars in 1869. That was half a cowboy's monthly salary.

When cowboys reached the end of the trail in Abilene, Kansas, they fired off their guns in celebration. Abilene had been a crude little frontier village with a population of 300 when Joseph McCoy built his stockyards. It grew almost overnight into a booming city of 3,000 with more than a dozen saloons, dance halls, gambling houses, and hotels all trying to compete for the cowboys' wages. Pretty soon, Abilene earned a reputation for being the "wickedest and wildest town in the West." After all, what's a cattle drive without a cow-town celebration?

Tom Smith and Wild Bill Hickok became famous for their attempts to maintain order in Abilene — especially on the wild and dangerous Texas Street. In a time when cowboys did anything to stay alive, Wild Bill became known as the deadliest two-gun marshal on the Western frontier!

THE END OF THE TRAIL

More than six million cattle were herded out of Texas in the decades following the Civil War. In

1871 alone, around 700,000 cattle reached the Kansas railhead, ready to be shipped to points east.

But by 1886, cowboys no longer needed to drive their cattle to Kansas, because the railroads extended their lines deep into the heart of Texas. The golden age of the Chisholm Trail and the cowboy were over, but think of the legacy they left behind — they were tough survivors!

⑤ SURVIVING A BUFFALO HUNT WITH THE PLAINS INDIANS

In the mid-1800s, there were more than two dozen Plains Indian tribes—about 200,000 people in all—including the Blackfeet, Cheyenne, Sioux, and Comanche. Many of the tribes had been pushed out of the Eastern forests by European settlers and by bigger, stronger tribes with guns, like the Iroquois.

The tribes were new to this harsh environment and like all the heroes in extreme history, they did anything to stay alive! Surviving meant adapting to a new land where the main source of food was six and a half feet tall, weighed 2,000 pounds, and didn't like people very much. The Plains Indians were America's first big-game hunters!

THE BIG HUNT

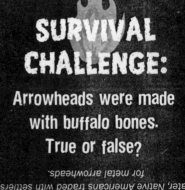

For the Plains Indians, hunting was never a sport — it was a matter of life and death. Not only was the American bison, or buffalo, their main source of food, but this giant, snorting beast also provided almost everything they needed to stay alive. Buffalo skins were used for clothes and shelter, hair was twisted into rope, horns were used for cups and spoons, and bones were transformed into weapons.

Hunting Buffalo the Native American Way

Hunting buffalo for a settler was easy — all he had to do was ride up on his horse and pull the trigger. But a Native American had to shoot his prey with a hand-made bow and arrow. Making arrows was always the first step in a buffalo hunt — and one arrow could take an entire day to make!

Rocks and leather

SURVIVAL CHALLENGE:

Arrowheads were made with buffalo bones. True or false?

Answer: True. Buffalo hump bones were used to make arrowheads. So was flint. Later, Native Americans traded with settlers for metal arrowheads.

were used as sandpaper to make arrowheads sharp. Then they were locked into the wooden shaft with buffalo-hide glue and buffalo back-strap sinew. Feathers made sure the arrow flew steadily. Great strength was required to draw an arrow with a powerful hunting bow.

Crow and Blackfeet hunters covered their bows with rattlesnake skins. Tribes decorated their arrows, and warriors added their own markings. Get caught with another guy's arrows and you were in big trouble!

Stalking the Herd!

Before the Spanish brought horses to North America, Native Americans hunted on foot. The big herds moved around all the time, and the Indians sometimes had a hard time catching them.

Did you know?

Plains Indians camouflaged their smell by rubbing things like sagebrush on their skin, then they draped themselves with buffalo robes or wolf hides to stalk their prey.

A direct hit with an arrow could kill a buffalo in eight to fifteen minutes. But an indirect hit only made it mad! A poorly shot arrow could cause a stampede and the whole tribe could go hungry. And sometimes the buffalo fought back. Female buffaloes, or cows, were known to charge hunters. Bulls, the male buffaloes, sometimes trampled. The hunters became the hunted.

One of the Plains tribes' best hunting methods was to drive a whole herd over a cliff! One warrior, camouflaged in a buffalo robe, would lead the herd to the edge of a cliff. Then other Indians would jump and shout behind the animals, causing a stampede. The terrified herd would stampede right over the side of the cliff — after the warrior in front dashed to safety at the last minute! Spears or bows and arrows finished off the animals that survived the fall. Hunters sometimes drove buffalo into deep snow or attacked herds at water holes where they were unable to get away.

Hunting on Horseback!

After horses were brought to North America, the Plains tribes became expert mounted hunters. Buffalo runs were wild, dangerous events. When a scout located a herd, a long line of hunters rode forward, being careful to stay downwind. At the signal, the warriors charged the herd at full gallop, guiding their horses with their knees.

Holding his bow in his left hand and a whip to urge his horse forward in his right, a hunter went after his target! As he closed in, the warrior aimed for the animal's lungs. If an arrow didn't go deep enough, the hunter might pull it out and use it again.

A buffalo can outrun a man on a horse and has more stamina. To stop dinner from getting away, you had to be a good shooter. A hunter could hope to get only three arrows off in a really short span of time.

Once an arrow hit its mark, the hunter took off after another buffalo. A well-trained horse knew

EXTREME SURVIVAL

The Plains-style bows were often more effective than muskets! A skilled warrior could shoot a stream of arrows faster than a man with a musket could reload and fire.

exactly what to do, and a brave warrior could kill as many as four or five buffalo in one run!

After the Kill

The whole tribe took part in the feast that followed a successful buffalo hunt. After the kill, before they even carried the buffalo back to camp, the hunters cut out the liver and ate it raw. They believed it gave them strength. As soon as the hunt was over, the women and children of the tribe joined the warriors to help cut up the buffalo and bring it back to camp. It was considered a real treat to eat the heart, kidneys, and brains while they were still warm!

The rest of the meat was roasted on campfires or boiled. Meat that could not be eaten right away was cut into strips and dried to make jerky. And the buffalo hides were tanned and cured to make robes, blankets, clothing, shields, bags, drums, and tepee covers.

But the Plains Indians didn't stop there. No part of the buffalo went to waste. Horns were used as spoons, cups, and toys. Tails became whips. Hoofs were turned into rattles or boiled to make glue, teeth became necklaces, and fat was used to make candles and soap.

Even the buffalo droppings were valuable. On the treeless plains, the Native Americans had an endless supply of dried buffalo dung. These "buffalo chips" burned slowly and made a hot fire.

And last but not least, buffalo bladders and stomachs were emptied and washed, then blown up like balloons. After drying in a tree for about a day, the bladder or stomach was a strong, tight water carrier!

Smoking a pipe filled with wild tobacco was the traditional way to end a buffalo hunt. It was also the Native American way to celebrate a victory in battle.

PLAINS INDIAN WARRIORS

Plains Indian men earned respect from the members of their tribes. They were seen as strong buffalo hunters, but their real glory came if they were brave warriors in battle. Warriors believed that war paint kept them safe in battle.

Sacred Stories

Although the Plains Indians didn't have a written language, they used paint to decorate their clothes, their tepees, and their battle shields with sketches showing the battles they had fought. Paint was never more important than when used to paint themselves in preparation for battle.

Many different colors of paint were used, made from everyday materials the Indians found in the world around them. Black paint could be made with boiled-down buffalo blood mixed with burnt willow twigs and buffalo or bear grease.

Old battle wounds were outlined in red to scare the enemy! Red was the most sacred color because it was the color of the people and the earth. The warriors first smeared their bodies with buffalo fat, then rubbed on the color.

Counting Coup

Today, taking someone's scalp would seem like a pretty gruesome war game. But the Plains Indians believed that when you took someone's scalp, you took his spirit and his soul, which protected you and your family in the next world. Scalps were displayed in camp and even worn in battle — to scare off the enemy, of course!

Plains Indians valued bravery more than killing. The greatest honor came from touching an enemy during battle — without actually killing

SURVIVAL CHALLENGE:

Horses were also painted to protect them during battle. True or false?

Answer: True!

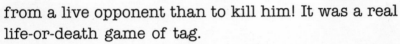

him! Known as counting coup (*coup* is the French word for "blow"), this was considered most courageous because it was more dangerous to escape from a live opponent than to kill him! It was a real life-or-death game of tag.

Returning warriors, like returning hunters, sang and danced and recited war chants. Warriors told of their brave deeds in camp and received an eagle feather for each successful coup. The more feathers they had in their war bonnets, the braver they appeared in the eyes of their tribe and in the eyes of their enemies.

As European settlers came to the Great Plains, the buffalo herds began to disappear. Traders wanted buffalo robes and tongues for markets in the East and pioneers traveling west in covered wagons shot the animals for food. One hunter — Buffalo Bill Cody — killed 4,280 animals in seventeen months to feed railroad construction crews. Soon buffalo hunting became a popular sport.

By the end of the nineteenth century, the buffalo had been driven to near extinction. The Plains Indians had been forced to live on reservations and their proud way of life came to an end, but their noble lifestyle will never be forgotten.

DOOM, DEATH, AND DANGER: THE ULTIMATE SURVIVAL CHALLENGE

Now that you've read about some of history's most dangerous and exciting survival stories, test your knowledge and see if you have what it takes to stay alive!

1. On an 1812 battleship, what did sailors spread on deck before battle?

a. sawdust

b. salt water

c. sand

2. In prehistoric times, who first discovered fire?

a. *Homo sapiens*

b. *Homo erectus*

c. *Homo habilis*

3. What did Lewis and Clark trade for food in North Dakota?

a. battle-axes

b. canoes

c. portable soup

4. Cowboys had to be experts with

a. a slingshot

b. a lariat

c. a pistol

5. What early weapon did <u>Homo sapiens</u> invent?

a. the rifle

b. the spear

c. the slingshot

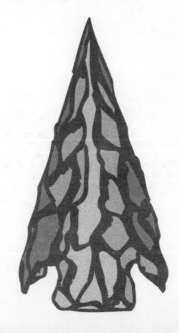

6. What was the Plains Indians' best hunting tool?

a. the bow and arrow

b. the musket

c. the spear

7. What was the worst job for a cowboy on the Chisholm Trail?

a. cook's assistant

b. point man

c. drag rider

8. Civil War soldiers were most often wounded by

a. bayonets

b. minié balls

c. knives

9. Powell's Colorado River expedition traveled through

a. the Grand Canyon

b. Indian Territory

c. the Rocky Mountains

10. Plains Indians made canteens out of what part of the buffalo?

a. horns

b. bladders

c. skulls

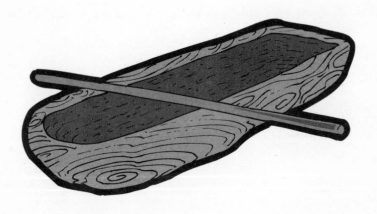

ANSWERS TO DOOM, DEATH, AND DANGER: THE ULTIMATE SURVIVAL CHALLENGE

Answers: 1. c 2. b 3. a 4. b 5. c 6. a 7. c 8. b 9. a 10. b

SCORECARD:

If you answered more than seven questions correctly, you're a survivor! You have what it takes to stay alive in extreme history!

If you answered more than five questions correctly, you need to brush up on your survival skills. In a battle between you and nature, nature just might win!

If you answered four or fewer questions correctly, you're toast! Seriously, it's time to bone up on your survival skills!

GLOSSARY

Ancestor: a person from whom you are descended.

Blockade: to block an enemy's land or territory with troops or warships to keep out supplies.

Bone Marrow: a tissue, made of fat cells or red blood cells, found inside most bones.

Carronade: a gun that fired large ammunition at a short range that was used on warships.

Expedition: a journey taken for a specific purpose.

Hardtack: a hard biscuit or cracker.

Lariat: a long rope used with a running noose to catch livestock.

Portage: to carry boats overland from one body of water to another or around an obstacle (such as rapids).

Rapid: a part of a river where the current is very fast and the surface is choppy.

Shipwright: a ship's carpenter.

Sinew: a tendon, especially one used as a cord or a thread.

Tallow: melted-down animal fat used for soap, candles, and lotions.